MW00984879

POCKETBOOKS
by BroadStreet

100
Days of
Strength
F O R
Women

BroadStreet

BroadStreet Publishing Group, LLC.
Savage, Minnesota, USA
Broadstreetpublishing.com

100 Days of Strength for Women
© 2024 by BroadStreet Publishing®

9781424569182
9781424569199 eBook

Typesetting and design by Garborg Design Works | garborgdesign.com
Editorial services by Michelle Winger | literallyprecise.com

Printed in China.

24 25 26 27 28 29 30   7 6 5 4 3 2 1

I can do everything through Christ, who gives me strength.

PHILIPPIANS 4:13 NLT

Introduction

Is mounting tension and stress sapping you of your strength? Do you lack motivation and excitement to live each day to the fullest?

This pocketbook devotional encourages you to spend time with your Creator, drawing strength from his never-ending supply. As you reflect on these devotions, Scriptures, and prayers, you will be marked by truth and motivated to embrace all that God has for you. Through him, even in your weakest moments you are radiant and strong. Take courage in God's love for you and walk in confidence as you rely on him to renew and refresh you. As you spend time in his presence, he will fill you with peace and hope.

Rest Secure

I keep my eyes always on the LORD.
With him at my right hand, I will not be shaken.
Therefore my heart is glad and my tongue rejoices;
my body also will rest secure.

PSALM 16:8-9 NIV

No matter where you are, God is there. While there may be times you ache to hide from him in your shame, he is a constant presence. The beautiful thing about his omnipresence is that you have a steady and consistent companion who is always ready to help in times of trouble.

You have no reason to fear the things that the world may throw your way. You've got the best protector of all at your side! Are you asking for his help in times of worry and woe, or are you turning inward to try to solve your problems? Let God be your refuge. Nothing is too big or too small for him. Even in your darkest hours, you can know true joy because he is your guardian.

God, I take my cares and distress and cast them on you. I know that you can handle them for me. I rest secure in you.

DAY 2

Set Apart

"Before you were born I set you apart."

JEREMIAH 1:5 NIV

Nobody is an accident or an afterthought. The Lord has carefully crafted every person uniquely. He loved each individual before they were even born because he planned in his heart and mind exactly how they were meant to be.

Sometimes you may try to run away from how the Lord created you and from the calling he has placed on your life, but as you search for peace to accept who you are and how you were formed, you can have confidence that the Lord truly knows you. He knew you before the world began to hurt and influence you, and he knows how to restore you as well.

God, thank you for making me special and for setting me apart to do something specific for you. Help me to trust you as I walk in your calling for me.

Different Gifts

In his grace, God has given us different gifts for doing certain things well. So if God has given you the ability to prophesy, speak out with as much faith as God has given you.
ROMANS 12:6 NLT

What benefit is it if someone gives a child a gift, but that child never opens it or uses it? God has given each person natural abilities, talents, and spiritual gifts. He wants to teach them how to use them and what they are for. With the faith that you have, he asks you to step out in your gifts. In time your faith will grow.

Imagine if the child who received the gift only wanted to play alone. God's great plans for giving gifts includes serving and encouraging the entire body of believers. He has given each one a special position in his family and the tools needed to play their part well. Your gifts are not for you alone but to be used to help others.

God, give me the faith to step out and use the gifts you have given me. I want to use them to bless others.

Chosen Ones

*You are a chosen people, a royal priesthood, a holy nation,
a people for God's own possession, so that you may
proclaim the excellencies of Him who has called you out of
darkness into His marvelous light.*

1 PETER 2:9 NASB

On occasion, you may need a little nudge for all
the pieces of your disposition to fall into alignment
with God's. Today's nudge is a grand reminder of your
identity in the body of Christ. You are a holy priest
serving the living God! He is risen, and you are his.
Because of this, you walk in his light, and you shepherd
others into the light as well.

Sometimes, it is difficult to get rid of the grumpy
feelings of the day. It seems okay to have a lower
opinion of yourself or your circumstances (and maybe
even other people). But the truth is that God's opinion
should be your opinion, and you can shout that in
everything you do. Priests carry a message to the
people. What message are you carrying today?

*God, thank you for choosing me to be a priest for you.
Show me how to share the good news of your Son with
everyone I interact with.*

God has given
each person the tools
needed to play their
part well.

DAY 5

A Genuine Love

Love each other with genuine affection
and take delight in honoring each other.
ROMANS 12:10 NLT

One of the most difficult things to do is to love
someone who doesn't want to be loved. To love those
who push you away every time you try to help, those
who are difficult, and those who are maybe even a little
mean is discouraging, defeating, even costly.

Genuine love keeps showing up. It continues
to extend a hand of grace. It serves in every capacity
possible. It sees the whole person. Sometimes the
hardness of a person is just a mask. Often those
difficult people need to know deep down inside that
they are worth the effort.

Father, help me to show genuine love to those who are
diffcult. Give me grace as I reach out with your love and
kindness.

DAY 6

Written

*A person may have many ideas
concerning God's plan for his life,
but only the designs of his purpose
will succeed in the end.*

PROVERBS 19:21 TPT

Your future, just like your past, is in the hands of
God. You were not an afterthought or a disposable
extra detail. In fact, you were created for a very specific
part in God's family, and you are irreplaceable in the
eyes of the Lord. He made you from the outpouring of
his love, and by his design you came to be.

During the hard days, remember that God has a
purpose. Every one of your days are known by him and
destined for you even before your life began. The point
of the hard days is not to just move you to the good
days. There are incredible lessons to be learned and
insights to be gleaned from every day you are given.

*God, thank you for each day. Whether pleasant or difficult,
I can choose to walk through the day with joy and
appreciation.*

DAY 7

Busyness

"Come away by yourselves to a secluded place and rest a while." (For there were many people coming and going, and they did not even have time to eat.)
MARK 6:31 NASB

Life is so full that you may have difficulty finding time to spend with Jesus. So much demands your attention, it can be hard to find time to consecrate a portion of your day to God. He who has existed for eternity is not bound by time. Because he is outside of time, time does not limit him the way it limits you. When you take even a few sacred minutes to spend in his presence, he can meet you there and download deep truths to your heart.

In the days you feel you don't even have time to eat, ask God to give you the grace to find a few moments to slip away alone in his presence. God will speak volumes to a heart that is open to his truth—even over the hustle and bustle of your busiest days.

God, I admit there are times when I am really busy. Help me to prioritize spending time with you, so I can rest and recharge.

DAY 8

Heart Truth

O Lord, who shall sojourn in your tent?
He who speaks the truth in his heart.
PSALM 15:1-2 ESV

Thoughts need coaching because most of the time, they will derail. It is natural to become self-focused. When you do, insecurities and fears can subconsciously be strengthened. It's important to pause throughout the day and take stock of what you have given your mind to.

There is great value in actively controlling your mind. It is critical to speak the truth to your heart. Don't be discouraged when you see that you aren't walking closely with God. View it as a revelation from God to help you correct your course. He will give you the strength you need to align your mind with his truth.

Father, speak your truth into my heart, and help me to
listen to it closely. You have given me so much, and I am
grateful.

"*I will strengthen you and help you.*"

ISAIAH 41:10 NIV

DAY 9

Walk Wisely

Be very careful, then, how you live—not as unwise but as wise, making the most of every opportunity, because the days are evil.

EPHESIANS 5:15-16 NIV

Paul had been beaten, shipwrecked, stoned, imprisoned, and homeless. He was well aware that any day could be his last. Although you may not have been beckoned by death as often as he, you also do not know when your life will end.

Your time on earth is not just short, it is also filled with evil attempts. Everywhere you look, unwise people live for themselves and reject the grace of God. Let your life be led by the wisdom that comes from God so you can be pleasing to him and an example to others. When you live like this, you can make the most of every opportunity to witness to others.

God, thank you for the reminder to live for you each and every day. I want to walk in your wisdom and truth no matter what it costs me.

Vulnerability

He gives you more grace. That is why Scripture says:
"God opposes the proud
but shows favor to the humble."

JAMES 4:6 NIV

Some of the most substantial and ultimately wonderful changes in life come from moments of vulnerability: laying your cards on the table and letting someone else know how much they really mean to you. Vulnerability takes one key ingredient: humility. And humility is not easy. Isn't it sometimes easier to pretend that conflict never happened than to face the fact that you made a mistake and wronged another person? It's not easy to humble yourself and fight for resolution in an argument—especially when it means admitting your failures.

Who are you in the face of conflict? Do you avoid apologizing? Does your pride get in the way of vulnerability, or are you willing and ready to humble yourself for restoration? God says that he will give favor and wisdom to the humble.

God, I know you want me to be vulnerable and humble as I seek to restore relationships with those around me. Help me to be patient as I work through the healing process.

DAY 11

Faith or Sight

We are always confident and know that as long as we are at home in the body we are away from the Lord. For we live by faith, not by sight.

2 CORINTHIANS 5:6-7 NIV

It's easy to demand a lot of God. "God, I'd like this house," "God, this is my dream job," "I'm so ready to have a husband," and then you wait in expectation. You wait for him to do the impossible. You wait for him to give you the desires of your heart. Because if he does, then he is most definitely all-powerful. If he does, he heard your cry and answered. If he does, he loves you. This is living by sight.

In 2 Corinthians it says to live by faith, not sight. Don't doubt God. Living by faith is giving up any control you thought you had, and sitting in the passenger seat in eager anticipation of where God is taking you.

God, I want to live by faith and not sight. Help me to let go of unfulfilled desires. I believe that your purpose for me is great. You want only the best for me.

DAY 12

Unexpected Angels

The LORD hears good people when they cry out to him,
and he saves them from all their troubles.

PSALM 34:17 NCV

Sometimes your rescue can come in the form of another person. You cry out to God and ask him for help, but you shouldn't presume to know exactly how he is going to help you. God has humanity in his image and can express himself through people with their kind acts, words of encouragement, and often a great piece of advice or wisdom.

Thank God today for the people he has put in your life and the unexpected ways he can use them to encourage you. Thank him for revealing himself to you through others. Thank him that you can be part of the healing and grace he longs to share with the broken world.

Thank you, God, for the people you have put in my life
to encourage me in my walk and to help me through my
troubles.

Genuine love
keeps showing up.

Showers of Blessings

"Fear not, for I am with you;
be not dismayed, for I am your God;
I will strengthen you, I will help you,
I will uphold you with my righteous right hand."
ISAIAH 41:10 ESV

Some days your stress levels may leave you feeling like a rubber band that has been stretched to the limits—like you might snap at any time. Have you discovered the best place to get the strength you need?

You might not have time to sit down to read the Bible, but maybe you could play an audio one. The promises from God's Word will soak into your weary soul if you let them. Pray as you fold laundry. Play praise and worship music. The precious words of the songs will shower you with blessings as they tell about God's power and comfort and how he's always with you.

God, when I am carrying heavy burdens, help me to remember that your showers of blessings are available to me in so many ways. Teach me how to get my strength from you in those moments.

DAY 14

Tears on My Pillow

*Weeping may tarry for the night,
but joy comes with the morning.*

Psalm 30:5 esv

If you've lost someone close to you, your grief may be so deep that it's hard to catch your breath. You wonder if you'll ever smile again or how you'll make it through the weeks and months ahead. But you will. Cling to Jesus. His love will ease the pain like nothing else can.

Life will be different without the one you love, but the sun will shine again. You will smile, and you will laugh again. God will not leave you comfortless, and he will be enough for all that you're going through. As he has promised, he will give you rest—sweet rest—and joy will come in the morning.

God, when grief overwhelms me, help me to turn to your promises. I want to claim them as my own and believe that joy is coming in the morning.

DAY 15

Healthy Trees

Like trees planted in the Temple of the LORD,
they will grow strong in the courtyards of your God.
PSALM 92:13 NCV

Take a moment to reflect on a time when you
felt you were giving the best of yourself. You may be
thinking of times when you were utilizing your gifts
and talents and could witness your positive influence in
others around you. You may not have to reflect back far,
or you could be wondering where those times went!

Jesus describes himself as the vine. If you are being
nourished from that source, you will produce fruit. In
the times you feel like you are not flourishing, it may be
that the Father needs to do some necessary pruning—
for the health of both the branch and the whole vine.

Father, thank you that you want to prune me so I can
grow and produce good fruit. I am encouraged that you
want to use me even though it is sometimes difficult to give
my very best.

Approach God

In him and through faith in him we may approach God with freedom and confidence.

EPHESIANS 3:12 NIV

The access you have to approach God in prayer comes from Christ's sacrifice for your sins. You have been made pure and clean, so you can freely approach him. The confidence you have to come before him is because of your faith in Christ's sacrifice. He died for you, purified you, established your faith, and invited you to approach him.

None of what God did for you was by your merit; it is your free gift of salvation. This means you have relationship with the Savior. You can only choose to respond and embrace it. As you come before him in prayer, recognize that even the right to approach God is a gift from him. Thank him for breaking down the divide. Praise him for the freedom and confidence he has filled you with. Remember how blessed you are to serve a God who desires relationship with his creation.

God, help me to come confidently to you, approaching you with freedom because Jesus has made a way for me to stand before you.

God is the strength of my heart and my portion forever.

PSALM 73:26 ESV

Mindset of Christ

In your relationships with one another, have the same mindset as Christ Jesus: Who, being in very nature God, did not consider equality with God something to be used to his own advantage and being found in appearance as a man, he humbled himself by becoming obedient to death— even death on a cross!

PHILIPPIANS 2:5-6, 8 NIV

The attitude Christ bore was one of servanthood and sacrifice. His humble obedience is meant to serve as a model for you to replicate. If the King of the universe is willing to overlook his grandiose rights for the sake of love, then you can also partake in serving others in the relationships God has given you.

Whatever your current calling, you know you are walking with a God who understands. He can help you embrace the relationships he has given you with the same attitude he has for others. You can love others the way he has loved you when you do it through his strength.

God, when I find myself in situations that require Christlike servanthood, help me to embrace them with a humble and obedient mindset.

Compassion and Justice

*The LORD longs to be gracious to you;
therefore he will rise up to show you compassion.
For the LORD is a God of justice.
Blessed are all who wait for him!*

ISAIAH 30:18 NIV

The beautiful blending of God's compassion and justice is what gives the hope that he will amend everything in his timing. You may be longing for his justice now, but he compassionately holds back his judgment a while longer.

This same compassion forgave your sin and showed grace when you were worthy of death. God's amazing grace lifts you back up. Wait patiently for the Lord because his grace is abounding and his fairness is exact.

Thank you for your compassion and justice, God. You will make everything right in your time. I believe this is true, and I walk in confidence of it.

Miraculous

You are the God who does miracles;
you have shown people your power.
PSALM 77:14 NCV

The Bible is full of exciting accounts of power, healing, and resurrection. You might find yourself wishing that you had been there when the fire of God fell upon Elijah's sacrifice, or when the storm was stilled by a voice, or when the blind man gained sight, or when Lazarus stepped out of the tomb.

God is clear that miracles didn't stop when the Bible ended. His power isn't limited by the ages, and he is just as omnipotent today as he always has been. Approach this day with hope in your heart. God is a God of the impossible.

God, I have faith to believe that the miracles you performed in the Bible can still be done today. Thank you for your amazing power and faithfulness.

True Life

This is how God showed his love to us:
He sent his one and only Son into the world
so that we could have life through him.

1 JOHN 4:9 NCV

The Bible is so clear that Jesus is God's Son
and that true life is found only through him. It says
that God sent him, implying that he came here
from elsewhere. Jesus was not simply born here like
everyone else; he existed before time with God and as
God. They are one together and divine in nature.

Being sent also indicates that Jesus had been given
a mission. He was not on a casual visit to earth but on
an assignment to demonstrate God's love for mankind,
his complete dominance over death and all evil realms,
and to free everyone from bondage by taking it on
himself.

God, thank you that your love is more than a feeling. You
demonstrated your love through powerful actions.

He who has
existed for eternity
is not bound
by time.

Life in Christ

*If there is any encouragement in Christ, any comfort in
love, any participation in the Spirit, any affection and
sympathy, complete my joy by being of the same mind,
having the same love, being in full accord and of one mind.*
PHILIPPIANS 2:1-2 ESV

The cause and effect outlined in these verses
speak to the relevance of the love of Christ and,
as a consequence, Christian love. Christ is your
encouragement and his love comforts you. The
Holy Spirit guides you and is involved in your life.
Anyone who has accepted Christ as their Savior is well
acquainted with his affection and sympathy.

You can experience joy, love, and have a similar
mindset as other believers which unites you under
Christ. This letter was written to the Philippians so
long ago, and yet the same truths are evident today.
Praise God for being the completion of your love, joy,
and unity.

*God, help me to be of the same mind with those in your
body. Help me not to create division but to seek peace in the
way I handle my relationships.*

Sweet Dreams

*Fully awake, he rebuked the storm and shouted to the sea,
"Hush! Calm down!" All at once the wind stopped howling
and the water became perfectly calm.*
MARK 4:39 TPT

The wind picked up and seemed to come from
all directions. The boat began to rock side to side and
pitch forward and back. Lightning lit the pitch-black
sky, thunder rumbled, and rain pelted. The disciples
should've been sleeping, but they were so anxious
about the weather that they actually thought they
might lose their lives that night.

Stressful situations and events can cause
temporary insomnia. The disciples worried about a
violent storm and couldn't close their eyes. You may
also worry about storms in your life. Troubles might
surround you, but Jesus knows they exist, and he will
never leave nor forsake you. He is right by your side.
He can calm your anxiousness and allay your fears.

*God, when the storms of life come, please help me to trust
that you are with me. You will take care of me through it
all. You can calm my fear and anxiety with just one word.*

Look Up

*Let us run with endurance
the race God has set before us.*
HEBREWS 12:1 NLT

The writer of Hebrews compares the Christian journey to that of running a race. When you run a race, particularly a long one, you need perseverance especially when it gets hard. Races often begin feeling quite manageable, but inevitably there comes a point when completing the race seems not only daunting but perhaps impossible.

When this happens, your eyes might rest on the monotony of watching one foot after the other slowly propel you forward. The distance gained is almost imperceptible. However, when you look up toward your goal, you become reinvigorated. If you watch the ground or look behind you, you'll grow weary. Fix your eyes on God, and he will give you all the strength you need.

God, help me to lift my eyes to you when I become weary. I want to look at the end prize and continue to endure with you by my side.

Burning the Candle

*In vain you rise early
and stay up late,
toiling for food to eat—
for he grants sleep to those he loves.*

PSALM 127:2 NIV

There are days where you might wake up a little more sluggish, with a little less energy and positivity about the day. That can feel kind of empty: a gap you're hoping to fill.

The great thing about the God you serve is that in him can be complete. He can be the gap filler. As you sit with him, his light begins to burn brighter. When it's hard to get out of bed because you feel anxious or worried about the day ahead, ask God for the energy and strength to face another day. He will give you what you need.

God, sometimes I feel like I am burning the candle at both ends. Call me away to spend time with you, so I can rest in your goodness and gain strength from your presence.

The Lord is my strength and my song; he has become my salvation.

EXODUS 15:2 CSB

Well Timed

Everyone enjoys giving great advice.
But how delightful it is to say the right thing
at the right time!
PROVERBS 15:23 TPT

There are situations in life where you feel lost for words. Often this is in moments of deep grief, sudden shock, or extreme surprise. Overwhelming emotions can be hard to express, and when someone shares these emotions, you might not know how to reply. The Bible speaks a lot about being slow to speak, so God doesn't expect you to know what to say immediately.

An appropriate response to someone doesn't have to be quick, it's just good if it's timely. The next time you're at a loss for words, give yourself time to think and pray about a response. There's wisdom in letting the Holy Spirit guide you with encouraging words. Think of the joy you can bring to someone, perhaps not instantly, with the right words.

God, please help me to listen to you when I am looking for something encouraging to say. Show me when it's time to speak and when it's time to be quiet.

DAY 26

Peaceful Sleep

I lie down and sleep;
I wake again, because the LORD sustains me.
PSALM 3:3-4 NIV

There is always something to worry about, isn't there? Whether it's health, finances, relationships, or details, there are many unknowns in life that can easily keep you worrying. What if you could trust completely that God would take care of you and your loved ones. God is your rock, and he alone will sustain you.

There will be many unknowns in your life. There will be moments when the rug feels as though it's been pulled out from under you, and there is nothing you can do. In the moments you can't control, you can trust. You can rest your soul, your mind, and your body in the hands of the one who has the power to sustain you.

God, thank you for sustaining me. You are the only one who can bring me peace when the world around me is unsteady or unknown. I rest in you today.

Overcome the World

"I have told you these things, so that in me you may have peace. In this world you will have trouble. But take heart! I have overcome the world."

JOHN 16:33 NIV

There is no evil in this world that Christ has not already overcome. He has accounted for everything that may happen and guarantees that you can overcome it through his power. Take heart and have confidence knowing that you also have secured victory because of Jesus' resurrection.

God has related his plan to you so you have peace knowing that your future with him is guaranteed. Regardless of what terrible situations you face in this life, they will pass. Christ's kingdom is lasting and his victory is forever.

Thank you, Father, for helping me overcome trouble. You help me through the trials of this life and show me what wonderful things lay ahead in your kingdom.

DAY 28

Power without Limit

To him who is able to do immeasurably more than all we ask or imagine, according to his power that is at work within us, to him be glory in the church and in Christ Jesus throughout all generations, for ever and ever! Amen.

EPHESIANS 3:20-21 NIV

There is only so much you can accomplish in your own strength. You plow through your tasks, and you can get a lot done. But you are limited in your power.

God has no limit to what he can do! If you ask him to work in your life, there's no stopping the amazing things that will happen. You can accomplish more than you'd ever think to ask for. The best part is that he wants to do it for you. It's not a chore for him or another task to cross off his list so that you'll stop pestering him. He delights in showing you his power.

God, I want to ask you for bigger, bolder things. Give me the supernatural ability to accomplish all that you want me to do. Your power is without limit, and I am honored to be part of your great plan.

Some of the
most substantial
changes in life come
from moments of
vulnerability.

My Sheep

"I am the good shepherd.
The good shepherd lays down his life for the sheep."

JOHN 10:11 NIV

There is something soothing about the thought of sheep and shepherds, unless of course you are the one tending the sheep. Wouldn't it be nice at the end of a day to gather all your cares and leave them inside a pen to stay put for the night? Like scattered sheep, tasks leap through your mind. Shepherding is hard work. Herding your daily strivings into a safe and protected place and depositing them there would be lovely.

Jesus is the only way into the sheepfold. He is the only gate, and that knowledge provides comfort and peace. He gave his Word to guide you. When the cares of life scatter through your nights like restless leaping sheep, God wants you to remember who blocks the doorway. No one guards and protects like he does.

God, I give you all my bothersome cares today. I leave them with you and lay down to rest.

Hiding

Where can I go from your Spirit?
Where can I flee from your presence?
PSALM 139:7 NIV

These words were probably very similar to the ones Adam and Eve used in the garden when they were ashamed of their disobedience. It's how you feel when you are ashamed of something that you've done wrong. You want to hide and don't want to be found!

It's okay to feel bad about doing the wrong thing and to feel guilty about making a wrong decision. But you can't live in that guilt, and you can't hide forever. God already knows where you are. He is seeking restoration. His Spirit is already with you. If you are trying to run from him, it's a losing battle! Instead, surrender to him and let his grace bring you joy.

God, now is a perfect time to run to you. You call me out of my hiding and remove my shame. Thank you for covering my mistakes and leading me in the better way.

Exaltation

"Be still, and know that I am God.
I will be exalted among the nations,
I will be exalted in the earth!"
PSALM 46:10 ESV

This psalm is not an invitation to be lazy, but to heed God. Children of God are expected to work hard, be responsible, and fulfill their duties. They are not, however, to frantically attempt to force their way through life without heeding the Word of God or accepting his help and intervention.

When you rely on the power of your own strength, the temptation is to exalt yourself. God is your source of strength, and he alone is to be exalted in the earth. He may choose at times to honor you as a good father does, but you should be glorifying him and recognizing his leadership in your life.

God, I take time to listen to you today. You will lead and correct me because you see the bigger plan. I ask that you would be exalted in my life.

Approaching God

*This is the confidence we have in approaching God:
that if we ask anything according to his will, he hears us.*
1 John 5:14 niv

This verse should vanquish any idea Christians may have of God simply being a wishing well. Tossing prayers up to heaven and hoping for your own desires to be fulfilled is not how a lovestruck, servant-hearted believer is expected to approach the Almighty.

When your deepest desire is for the Lord and for all people to come to know him, you pray to him for directions and answers that align with his agenda. That does not mean you have to vet your prayers or leave out details and requests that matter to you. Everything comes under a covering of a mutual understanding that his master plan is what you are aiming at and hoping for above all else.

*God, I pray for your will to be done in me and in the world.
Help me to know what you want to see happen today.*

*He gives power
to the weak and
strength to the
powerless.*

Isaiah 40:29 NLT

Whatever Comes

*"I will be strength to him
and I will give him my grace
to sustain him no matter what comes."*
PSALM 89:21 TPT

This verse was God's promise to David when he chose him to be the king of Israel. You have the hindsight to know the mistakes and troubles that David went through. Scripture lays out David's story of blessing, sin, consequence, joy, battles, fear, and love.

David went through a lot in his life, and the truth of this verse prevailed. God gave him grace and sustained him no matter what came. Let this verse be your promise today. Trust God to shower you with grace that will sustain you through everything you face.

God, I ask you to be my strength today. I want to have confidence in you no matter what comes. You will give me grace and sustain me.

DAY 34

Life's Journey

He asked you for life, and you gave it to him—
length of days, for ever and ever.
Surely you have granted him unending blessings
and made him glad with the joy of your presence.

PSALM 21:4, 6 NIV

Though the words *fear* and *fright* are commonly associated with one another, they don't mean the same thing. Having a fear of the Lord means you respect him. It means you are in awe of him. He is, in fact, a God of great joy. When you seek to be fully in his presence, you can find that joy.

Our Father wants you to experience his joy. Unending blessings? Sign up for that! Shake off any old notions of dread or apprehension you may feel about being in his presence and seek the path of life he has set for you. He is a source of great delight.

Thank you, Father, for your unending blessings and joy.
You are so good to me, and I thank you that I don't have to
be afraid of you. I am in awe of you.

Self-Control

Better to be patient than powerful;
better to have self-control than to conquer a city.

PROVERBS 16:32 NLT

What benefit is it to conquer a city if the other city had better intentions? If the Lord were to select someone to do a job, would it not make more sense that he chooses the one who is willing to listen to him and patiently wait for his instructions over the one who is more powerful?

Your power and strength come from God as does your calling. Enacting skills he has given you brashly and arrogantly is unfitting for a child of God. He has equipped you in order to obey him. Having self-control and patiently waiting upon his instructions is of more worth than spoils from an entire city.

God, please show me how I can use my skills and talents for you. I want to be self-controlled and patient in the way that I handle tasks and people.

Rejoice

Rejoice in the Lord always.
I will say it again: Rejoice!
PHILIPPIANS 4:4 CSB

True joy is so much more than mere happiness. As a Christian, you rejoice because of the hope you have in Jesus. There will come a day when all your suffering and sorrows will be wiped away and you will finally be at home with your Lord. Understanding this powerful truth should fill you with a continual joy that is more real than your circumstances.

When Paul penned these words, he was in jail for being wrongly accused. Just prior to his imprisonment, he had been shipwrecked, bitten by a shark, and placed under house arrest. Yet because of how aware he was of his eternal inheritance, nothing was able to steal his joy.

God, help me choose to rejoice in hard circumstances and also throughout the mundane activities of life. I am grateful for the joy I have because of you.

Troubles might surround you, but Jesus knows they exist, and he will never leave you.

Unfathomable

Do you not know? Have you not heard?
The LORD is the everlasting God,
the Creator of the ends of the earth.
He will not grow tired or weary,
and his understanding no one can fathom.
ISAIAH 40:28 NIV

The Lord never grows weary of doing good, nor does he tire of loving you. He is the Creator of the universe, and he diligently upholds the world, governs it wisely, and judges it righteously. With vigor and strength, he provides for all his creation, from the birds to the grass to his beloved Church.

With an unfathomable understanding and infinite love that none can grasp, he cares for all needs out of his goodness. He understands you, considers your desires, and gives you a unique calling. He is majestic and his ways are perfect. He has crafted everything with care and consideration. His eyes are always on you, and he leads you in the path of righteouness.

Thank you, Father, for never growing weary of me! You understand me, and you stay close to me. Thank you for your neverending love.

Let Grace Win

If you bite and devour each other,
watch out or you will be destroyed by each other.

GALATIANS 5:15 NIV

Watching animals in the wild hunt, defend, and fight for territory can be brutal. You are not a wild animal, but it might pay to stop and think about whether you are acting like one. When you start to assume or say unkind things about people, it can be the start of an attack on character or a judgment call you may not know enough about to make.

God doesn't call you to be the judge of what others say or do, he wants you to have control of yourself. Instead of being ready to attack or defend your territory, you should be quick to forgive, try and understand others' perspectives, and stay out of the danger of judgment. Always let grace win. Let your heart be full of it, so it spills over into the way you treat others.

God, forgive me for speaking unfairly about others, and help me to forgive those who have wrongly accused me. You are the perfect judge, and I leave everything in your hands.

A Pilgrimage

Happy are the people whose strength is in you,
whose hearts are set on pilgrimage.

PSALM 84:5 CSB

This is a go, go, go culture. Keep running 24/7 as fast as you can. Do you have the courage to slow down? Or are you plagued by the fear of missing out? This fear grips you to take life more at the speed of a motocross race and less the way it was intended to be: a pilgrimage. An exodus out of bondage and into freedom. Out of darkness, into light. Out of death, into resurrection. A pilgrimage is a slower journey, not a race run at a remarkable speed.

You might run quickly for a couple reasons: you don't want to miss out, or you want to blaze past all the hard stuff. You won't be rewarded for how fast you obtain the prize, or how much you accomplished along the way. On this exodus, quality matters. Miss out. Say no. Go slower. Don't give in to the temptation to run. Walk with Christ, allowing him to mature you as you move.

God, sometimes I feel like I am moving too quickly. Help me to slow down and spend time resting in your presence. I want to gain my strength by being with you.

Beside Still Waters

He leads me beside still waters.

PSALM 23:2 ESV

The words of Psalm 23 are often featured on greeting cards and artwork. Have you wondered why God uses still waters as a picture of comfort? Have you ever been by a quiet stream? The surface is so clear it's like a mirror. It reflects the peaceful beauty of God's creation. The water draws you to it, and the stillness invites you to also be still, giving rest for your soul.

Can you think of anything that a stressed person could use more than calmness and restful silence? God knows what you need to restore and refresh you. It's hard to hear his words of comfort if you're zipping around, or if you're in turmoil and constant action. When you're still, you can hear God's soft whispers. And when he soothes your stress-filled soul, you won't lack for anything.

God, thank you for the quiet, comforting words in Psalm 23. I am grateful for your stillness that brings comfort and rest to my soul.

The Lord will
give strength to
His people;
The Lord will
bless his people
with peace.

PSALM 29:11 NKJV

DAY 41

Keeping a Secret

A gossip goes around revealing a secret,
but a trustworthy person keeps a confidence.
PROVERBS 11:13 CSB

You've been there before. A friend leans in and whispers, "Did you hear about what she did?" And something in you wants to know. To hear the scoop. To spread the word. You have to share what you know of others' downfalls and fallacies.

It might feel good in the moment to tear people down because then you are not alone in the many ways you fall short. But it is a lie. You were designed to lift others up. To be worthy of knowing a friend's secrets because you will keep the knowledge to yourself. The next time you are tempted to share what isn't yours to tell, take a deep breath and pause. Ask yourself if betraying a confidence is worth letting down a friend. Be the type of friend God has designed you to be.

God, help me to be a trusted friend who keeps confidences to myself. I want to treat my friends the way you treat me, covering them in love and grace.

DAY 42

Bless Someone

May he give you the desire of your heart
and make all your plans succeed.

PSALM 20:4 NIV

What a beautiful Scripture! May God give you
the desire of your heart and make your plans succeed.
This is a great verse for you, but could it also be for
someone else in your life? Think of someone in need of
encouragement today and choose to pray this blessing
over that person.

It might be your mother or father, someone you
know who has been unwell, perhaps it's the friend with
a new baby or someone who has just started a new
job. Whatever that person's situation is, pray that God
would make their plans succeed!

God, as I go about my day, please show me people who are
in need of encouragement. I want them to know that you
care about their success.

His Strength

Look to the LORD and his strength;
seek his face always.

PSALM 105:4 NIV

It may be your natural instinct to cry out to God in a panic and desperately search for him when you find yourself in crisis. However, you don't have to panic or feel distressed in the face of the unknown. You can just ask him for help and he will be faithful to meet you. His strength is readily available. You can know the joy of his presence and the comfort and stability of his faithfulness.

God calms your racing and anxious thoughts with truth. He offers you wisdom and direction in the middle of decision making. He pierces the darkness with his light. He fills you with gratitude and thanksgiving and renews your faith. He breathes bravery into your weak and timid soul.

Father, I draw my strength from you both in times of need and in times of peace. Thank you for always being ready to share your goodness with me.

DAY 44

Hope

May the God of hope fill you with all joy and peace as you trust in him, so that you may overflow with hope by the power of the Holy Spirit.

ROMANS 15:13 NIV

What differentiates hope from a wish? Think about the lottery. Does one hope to win or wish to win? How about a promotion, a pregnancy, or a proposal? Both hoping and wishing contain desire, but for wishing, that is where it ends. Hope goes deeper. The strong desire for something good to happen is coupled with a reason to believe that it will.

You can see then how vital hope is, and why it's such a beautiful gift. Desire without hope is empty, but together they bring joy, expectancy, and peace. When you put your hope in Christ, he becomes your reason to believe good things will happen.

God, you are my hope. I believe good things will happen because you are faithful.

In the moments
you can't control,
you can trust.

DAY 45

Righteous Answers

By awesome deeds you answer us with righteousness,
O God of our salvation,
the hope of all the ends of the earth
and of the farthest seas.

PSALM 65:5 ESV

What have you been asking God for lately? It could be healing from illness, prayer for someone close to you who is hurting, or maybe you just need a little help in your relationships. It is often said that God hears your prayers; yet you might feel like he has never answered.

God can seem far away and unconcerned with your requests and needs. These feelings, however, are not the truth. God is always very near to you. He knows your heart, he knows what you need, and he will answer. Trust him as you read this Scripture again and know that he will answer your prayers with amazing wonders and inspiring displays of power. Let this increase your faith today.

God, you are my hope that extends to the ends of the earth and farthest of seas. Help me to hold onto you today. You have all the answers I need.

A Place of Rest

The LORD is my shepherd; I shall not want.
He makes me lie down in green pastures.
PSALM 23:1 ESV

What is restful for you? Is there a place you like to go when you need to be refreshed? There's something special about enjoying the beauty of God's creation. While you sit and take it in, you can almost feel the stress seeping away from you.

When you discover the beauty of creation—a still lake, a canopy of leaves, a starry sky—a sweet peacefulness seeps into your souls. You find rest as you worship the author of beauty. Both your soul and body can be refreshed. Sometimes you don't have to get in your pajamas to find rest; you just need to look for Jesus. And when you find his fingerprints on the world he created, make it a priority to spend time with him there.

God, your creation is so restful. Help me to make it a priority to stop and enjoy it.

The Desire Beneath

Since we know he hears us when we make our requests,
we also know that he will give us what we ask for.
1 John 5:15 nlt

When birthdays or anniversaries are coming up, people often get asked what they want as a gift. You may be someone that answers that easily, or you might take a while. Eventually you have an answer of what you would like or even need, but you never really know if you are going to get it, and you often have to wait until that significant day to find out!

You can be confident that God hears you when you tell him what you want or need. Perhaps you haven't had the confidence to voice it, but he knows your heart anyway. Could you consider that God knows the true desire behind your requests, and that this real desire is what you end up getting? It's a thought that is worth pondering today.

Heavenly Father, I know you are listening. Today I ask you for the things I want. I trust that you know what I need most and that you will provide for me.

Praise through Circumstance

I have learned the secret of being content in any and every situation, whether well fed or hungry, whether living in plenty or in want. I can do all this through him who gives me strength.

PHILIPPIANS 4:12-13 NIV

When life is good, it is easy to praise God. *My life is full of blessings*, you think. He is so good to me! But what happens when life is hard? Do you continue to give him the glory when you're thrown curveball after curveball?

Regardless of your circumstance or situation, continue to give God the praises he so richly deserves. A life lived alongside Christ doesn't mean it will be one free of pain, discomfort, or tough times. But it does mean that you can find contentment in it anyway because you have him to turn to. Pray for contentment today, whatever your circumstance. There is no crisis that the Lord is not willing to walk you through. You can do anything with him at your side!

God, thank you for your compassion and help when my circumstances aren't ideal. I trust you to take care of me, and I praise you for it.

"The joy of
the Lord is
your strength."

Nehemiah 8:10 niv

Your Best Work

Whatever you do, work heartily, as for the Lord and not for men, knowing that from the Lord you will receive the inheritance as your reward. You are serving the Lord Christ.
Colossians 3:23-24 esv

When your work is difficult, mundane, or thankless, you can remember that everything you do is for the Lord. Out of appreciation and love for him, you embrace each day's tasks with joy because you serve the King! Even if your toils are for a difficult boss or unappreciative children, your calling comes from God and your rewards do as well. Put your best effort into your daily grind even if it seems to be devalued here on earth. It has always mattered to God.

When others attempt to destroy your efforts, undermine your work, or steal your success, continue to serve with your whole heart because that is what God has called you to. The end results are in his hands. You can trust him to bless your work. He is your reward.

Thank you, God, for the opportunity to serve you. You are my reward. I draw my strength from you.

DAY 50

Crown of Joy

*Those the L*ORD *has rescued will return.*
They will enter Zion with singing;
everlasting joy will crown their heads.
Gladness and joy will overtake them,
and sorrow and sighing will flee away.
ISAIAH 51:11 NIV

When the Lord rescued the Israelites out of Babylon and led them back to their own land, there was great rejoicing and singing! Their sorrow was replaced by joy, for they had served in captivity for a long time. It was not the first time God had rescued them from slavery; Egypt was still fresh in their history. It also will not be the last time the Lord will rescue his people and lead them to their promised land.

When the Lord returns for his people again, they will finally enter his eternal promised land. Sorrow and crying will be replaced with everlasting joy and singing. God will never forget his children. He has always made a way for them to return to him.

God, thank you for always bringing me back to you. You have rescued me, and you continue to pursue me. I have joy because of you.

DAY 51

"Be strong and courageous and do the work. Don't be afraid or discouraged, for the LORD God, my God, is with you. He will not fail you or forsake you."
1 CHRONICLES 28:20 NLT

When the work before you is daunting, you may rush through it or stall out in the process. Jesus has an answer for that. He says he will not fail you or forsake you. To fail you would be to give you an answer or technique that does not work for what you are supposed to be doing. To forsake you would be to walk away from you in your time of need.

If you truly believe God has done either of these to you, you really need to sit in the quiet with your Bible and an open heart toward him. He promises that if you seek him fully, you will find him. In doing this, you will eradicate faulty thinking and get back on your feet with the strength and courage to do what had once seemed daunting. Jesus is with you!

God, give me strength to believe that you have my best in mind. You will not forsake me, and you will not fail me. I trust you today.

DAY 52

Compassionate and Gracious

"The LORD, the LORD, the compassionate and gracious God, slow to anger, abounding in love and faithfulness."
EXODUS 34:6 NIV

Each day you walk with the Lord, your hope should be to mature in him. The more you learn about his character, his goodness and compassion, his mercy and his love, the more you want to be like him. The more you know of God and his lovingkindness, the more convinced you become to better yourself. To soften your heart. To be like him.

What more could you want in your heart of hearts than to be compassionate and gracious? Slow to anger? Abounding in love and faithfulness? Looking into your own character is not always enjoyable. You may be ashamed of things you have said or done. God is faithful to forgive you. Take a courageous stand and declare, "Today is a new day. I will be compassionate and gracious to those I meet. I will be slow to anger. I will abound in love. I will be more like Jesus."

God, please show me how to be more compassionate. I want to be slow to anger and grow in my relationship with you.

Live in hope that
a day will come
where joy will
reign supreme.

DAY 53

Worthy

*You are worthy, our Lord and God, to receive glory and
honor and power, for you created all things, and by your
will they were created and have their being.*

REVELATION 4:11 NIV

Within the vision God gave to John, he saw
twenty-four elders before the throne of God. They
were declaring the truths written in this verse. From
God alone and for God alone do you exist and have a
purpose. You are not an accident or an afterthought.

Creator God designed this world with all its
wonder because it was his will. It is his will that you
live, and he is therefore worthy of the praise of your
life. All glory, honor, and power are his, for you are
nothing without him. Give him the honor he is due.
Demonstrate the gratitude that you feel. God created
you and gave you meaning. Uncover his purposes and
declare his praises, for it is why you were made!

*God, thank you for giving me a purpose in life. You deserve
all the glory and honor because you are the great Creator.*

His Story

*I will tell about the LORD's kindness
and praise him for everything he has done.*
ISAIAH 63:7 NCV

You have a story to tell. When you think back over the years, reflect on the things that revealed God's goodness, graciousness, and love. Perhaps it was an illness or healing, a relationship or a relationship breakdown, it might have been a joy or a disappointment in your career. God is right next to you in all the things life throws at you.

You may not have recognized him at the time, but hopefully you can attest to his kindness as you remember how you got through those times. This is your story, and just like the Israelites, it is worth telling and repeating. Your story is important, so be brave and speak it out!

God, thank you for your goodness, mercy, and kindness throughout my life. I want to share my story with those around me.

Another Gift

*Because he was full of grace and truth,
from him we all received one gift after another.*

JOHN 1:16 CSB

You know those perfect days? Your hair looks great,
you nail a work assignment (whether client presentation,
spreadsheet, or getting kids to nap at the same time),
you say just the right thing and make someone's day, and
then come home to find dinner waiting for you. It's good
upon good, blessing upon blessing.

Being a child of the Almighty gains you access
to that blessed feeling every day even when your
circumstances are ordinary or difficult. His love is so
full and his grace so boundless, that even a flat tire can
feel like a blessing if you let it.

*God, thank you for your grace that has been poured out on
me today. I am blessed by your continued gifts.*

DAY 56

Rebuilding

The Lord will rebuild Jerusalem;
there his glory will be seen.
PSALM 102:16 NCV

You probably have a lot of thoughts about your day ahead: grocery lists, appointments, trainings, or where you put those keys! You might be so consumed with your thoughts of all the details of the day that you forget to think on the greatness of God.

When you allow your thoughts of God to take over, you see your small concerns about the day fall away. Ask God to break through your stresses and help you concentrate on what matters the most. Thank him that in the times of deepest need he is the water of life you can draw your strength from.

God, thank you for your strength and encouragement to continue building when things seem chaotic and stressful. You are my source of refreshment.

Always let grace win.

Changing Seasons

He made the moon to mark the seasons;
the sun knows its time for setting.
PSALM 104:19 ESV

You will, undoubtedly, have various seasons in your life: seasons of longing and contentment, seasons of discouragement and joy, seasons of more and less. Being an adult means stretching into new ways of living, and this usually doesn't happen until the season hits.

Don't make excuses for why you can't do what God is calling you to do. Be brave! God will not move you into something without giving you the grace you need to make it through. The Lord has placed a calling on your life, and he will give you the courage to know that he is with you when he calls you to step forward.

God, thank you for changing seasons. Help me to identify the season I am in and ask you for the help I need to get through it.

DAY 58

Things Unknown

"Call to Me, and I will answer you, and show you great and mighty things, which you do not know."

JEREMIAH 33:2-3 NKJV

"If you're there God, give me a sign!" People have screamed this into the heavens many times throughout the years. You want to see something that will tell you that God is real and present. You want that experience that will bring heaven to earth and expel your doubt with a single lightning bolt. God is more than able to give you those miraculous signs, but he is so much more than an amazing experience.

God can show you things you don't know. Don't limit him to your experience and what you presently know of him and of life. He will show you great and mighty things if you ask him to. God is not limited by time, space, or human understanding. Put your hope and faith in him alone.

God, I know you are there. Show me the things you want me to know, and help me to trust that you are speaking to me.

DAY 59

Words Matter

Do not let any unwholesome talk come out of your mouths,
but only what is helpful for building others up according to
their needs, that it may benefit those who listen.

EPHESIANS 4:29 NIV

"Sticks and stones may break my bones, but words
will never hurt me." This often-quoted childhood rhyme
isn't true at all. Words do hurt. They matter. God has
called his children to build one another up instead of
tearing down. How you speak with others will define you.
Do your friends consider you trustworthy or incapable of
keeping a secret? Do you use your words as a weapon, or
are your conversations encouraging and helpful?

Choose your words and conversations carefully.
Take a moment to gather your thoughts before speaking
and especially before responding to someone else.
Don't return one mean statement with another. Being
kind in thought, word, and deed are qualities to aim for.

Father, please help me not to be critical of others. I want
my words to encourage and build people up instead of
tearing them down.

DAY 60

Listening to God

After the earthquake came a fire, but the LORD was not in the fire. And after the fire came a gentle whisper.
1 KINGS 19:12 NIV

A surprising study on parenting styles revealed that one of the best ways to get the attention of a child is to whisper. When instructing an important lesson, imparting it in a whisper helps the child to focus, to remember, and to act upon the information. Yelling or pontificating doesn't work as well. Taking the child onto your lap or sitting closely and softly speaking causes both memory and comprehension to improve.

Your heavenly Fathe wants to share so much with you. He wants to gather you up in his arms and give you strength. He longs to tell you of his unfathomable love. He wants to lighten your burdens and help you grow. Are you willing to listen to his still, small voice? Life is noisy. Slow down, be quiet, and listen to God. Take a deep breath, sink back into his arms, and allow him to feed your soul.

God, I want to listen to your voice. Help me to be still and wait for you in the quiet.

The Lord is
my strength and
my shield.
I trust him with
all my heart.
He helps me,
and my heart
is filled with joy.

PSALM 28:7 NLT

Confident Trust

Do not throw away this confident trust in the Lord.
Remember the great reward it brings you!
HEBREWS 10:35 NLT

After writing an entire book dedicated to validating and strengthening a Christian's confidence in Christ, the author issues this warning: do not lose it. Maintain your confidence and trust in God. In the end, it will be rewarded.

The best way to remain confident is by remembering the truth of God's Word. Immerse yourself regularly in it, so the subtle lies and twisting of truth that the world constantly bombards you with do not begin to corrupt your confidence. Hold fast to the Father and ask for wisdom to discern truth from the lies. Confidently stand on faith in God alone. He is the only way.

Father, I want to surround myself with truth. Help me to find the right avenues to do so. I look forward to the reward you have waiting for me.

DAY 62

Power

"You will receive power
when the Holy Spirit comes on you."
ACTS 1:8 NIV

After Jesus's ascension, he gave the promised gift of the Holy Spirit to the disciples. They were told to wait for this gift before they proceeded any further. Jesus knew it would be fruitless to attempt to carry out any exploits unless his followers were filled with his Spirit. As they waited, the Holy Spirit came and filled them with power. This was a power they lacked prior to this moment. It wasn't something they could conjure up on their own. Jesus wanted them to know that a new power would come.

That same power is there for all who ask. God hasn't given you a spirit of fear but one of power. You don't need your own power, God will give you his through the Holy Spirit.

Holy Spirit, I need your power to accomplish all that you are asking me to do. I don't want to lean on my own strength.

Accept Your Gift

Do not neglect the gift that is in you, which was given to you by prophecy with the laying on of the hands of the eldership. Meditate on these things; give yourself entirely to them, that your progress may be evident to all.

1 TIMOTHY 4:14–15 NKJV

Paul wrote to Timothy encouraging him to use his gift of teaching. Of what profit is it to simply possess gifts if you forgo using them? God has invested a unique set of traits in you to reflect himself and to play an intrinsic part in his plan.

God will teach you how to use your gifts and offer you opportunities to put them to use if you trust his leading and guiding. It is important that you refrain from becoming jealous of someone else's gift and praise God for the gifts he has given to you, learning to use them for his glory.

Thank you, God, for the gifts you have given me. Help me to use them to bless others, and help me to see the gifts those around me have. I want to encourage them in their gifts as well.

DAY 64

Poverty

*Being kind to the poor is like lending to the L*ord*,*
he will reward you for what you have done.
PROVERBS 19:17 CSB

People can be poor in many ways. You may not come across true poverty or see homeless people in your everyday life, but there are those who also suffer from poverty of joy, hope, and love. Some are hurting from their lack of being loved by someone or are suffering from despair.

Ask the Holy Spirit to show you the poor and find a way to bring grace into their situation. It might be practical help, a kind word, or an invitation to grab coffee. Let the grace that dwells in you be poured out on those around you and know that your heavenly Father will be overjoyed that you are sharing his love.

God, please help me to see the poverty in the people around me. Show me how I can lend to them in a way that brings honor to you.

Salvation tore the veil that separated you from the holiness of God.

DAY 65

Floodwaters

The LORD rules over the floodwaters.
The LORD reigns as king forever.
PSALM 29:10 NLT

Picture a season in your life where you were knee-deep in busyness, swallowed in sadness, or buried in exhaustion. Picture that season and how you looked, acted, reacted, and survived.

Now picture the King of the heavens and earth. See how he rules over the entire earth. This powerful God wants you to lean on him, and that seems easy to do when you understand just how great and mighty he is. If you have woken up feeling tired, lean on the strength of your Savior.

God, sometimes I feel weary and weak. Help me not to look somewhere else for strength but to rely on you instead. You are the only true source of power I need.

Cheerful Face

A joyful heart makes face cheerful,
but a sad heart produces a broken spirit.
PROVERBS 15:13 CSB

Real joy is lasting and is not deterred by circumstances, for it is caused by the hope you have in Jesus for your eternity. Since it is secured in that which will not fail, it cannot be broken by anything momentary. Joy is a gift that cannot be taken away. It helps you to find cheer when everything in your life seems to be in disarray.

When you give way to sadness and allow it to dictate your condition, your spirit will be broken and you can no longer find motivation to press forward. With eternity in your heart, you must cling to the joy that has been given to you. It will give you the strength and determination you need to overcome.

God, you know my every struggle. Help me to rely on your joy instead of allowing sadness to consume me.

Slaying the Giants

David said to the Philistine, "You come against me with sword and spear and javelin, but I come against you in the name of the LORD Almighty, the God of the armies of Israel, whom you have defied. This day the LORD will deliver you into my hands."

1 SAMUEL 17:45-46 NIV

Goliath had been taunting the Israelites for forty days, daring someone to come fight him. He was huge and terrifying, and nobody was brave enough to fight him except that shepherd boy who gathered five smooth stones from the stream.

Everyone has their giants: fear, stress, anxiety, depression to name a few. Giants are real and they can rock your world, stressing you to the limit. In those moments, do what David did: face the giant armed with God. That's where your power lies. Giants stress you, but God fights your battles. The next time you're weighed down with stress over situations that you can't fix, go to the one who can.

God, give me the courage to fight the giants that seem terrifying to me. I don't need to be afraid because you fight for me.

A New Creation

*If anyone is in Christ, he is a new creation. The old has
passed away; behold, the new has come.*

2 CORINTHIANS 5:17 ESV

Sarah's pajamas didn't feature images of playful
kittens, stylish shoes, or mugs of hot cocoa. Her
mattress wasn't six inches thick with cushy memory
foam on top. She didn't kiss her loved ones good-
night and then ease into sleep. Her pajamas were
prison-issued, the same color and style as all the
other prisoners. Her mattress was thin, and she was
far from loved ones. Every night when she stretched
out to sleep, all she could imagine was her mother's
brokenhearted face. She hadn't slept well since her
incarceration.

It's hard to sleep when guilt and shame are
crushing the breath from you. The God of grace and
mercy can make a new creation out of anyone. Shame
doesn't need to define you. Lean into the forgiveness of
God and allow him to make you new.

*God, thank you for forgiving me and for allowing my spirit
to rest from guilt and shame. You have made me new, and I
want to live with your peace in my heart.*

Desire without hope is empty, but together they bring joy, expectancy, and peace.

Little People

"The Son of Man came to seek and to save the lost."
LUKE 19:10 NIV

When your bodies are tired and your spirits match, it is easy to look at the great big world and feel very small. You try not to pay attention to numbers, but it's hard. You see how few likes you get on social media and watch promotions land on other people. You wonder why you are spinning your wheels. And sometimes it hits you: *I'm just a little person.*

The scope of your tiny place in a big world may make you feel insignificant, but little people have great value to Jesus. He came for all. He is your salvation and significance. Your great God has a divine purpose for you. Think about that today.

Thank you, God, for creating me for a specific reason and for sending Jesus to save me. I am not insignificant to you. I know this in my head but please help me feel it in my heart.

DAY 70

Refuge and Strength

God is your refuge and strength,
always ready to help in times of trouble.
So you will not fear when earthquakes come
and the mountains crumble into the sea.

PSALM 46:1-2 NLT

Since you have an eternal perspective and you know
that God is your help in times of trouble, you can have
confidence rather than fear when disaster strikes. When
others are overcome with worry or doubt, you continue
to focus on God and trust his hand will guide you.

Your strength and courage come from God. Even
if everything is crumbling down around you, you can
find refuge in him because he is greater than the world.
He is always prepared to offer his people comfort and
hope in times of tragedy. You don't need to worry
about the future like those who rely on themselves.
Don't seek shelter behind temporary shields because
God is your covering. He is your refuge and strength.

God, when catastrophes hit, help me to turn directly to you
and rely on you to be my refuge and strength. I don't need
to fear because you are holding me.

Sleep Like a King

*That night the king could not sleep; so he ordered the book
of the chronicles, the record of his reign, to be brought in
and read to him.*

ESTHER 6:1 NIV

Some nights you collapse into bed. Other nights
it's a long process of winding down and letting the day's
busyness melt away. You may have a bedtime routine
which helps you relax—a book, a hot bath, or a nice
cup of chamomile tea. Most would not choose King
Xerxes' strategy in the book of Esther, however the sheer
boredom of reading records would likely put you to sleep.

God uses even sleepless nights for his purposes.
Can it be God has your eyes open and mind alert for an
unseen reason? Perhaps someone needs intercession,
and you are awake for that purpose. God used the
king's sleepless night to express gratitude for a past
blessing, but ultimately his insomnia humiliated God's
enemies and saved a nation. His tedium of lists and
events proved to be part of a much greater plan.

*God, help me to be aware of the bigger plan you have in
mind. When I can't sleep, help me to connect with you for
direction and peace.*

Lulled to Sleep

A young man named Eutychus, sitting at the window,
sank into a deep sleep as Paul talked still longer.
ACTS 20:9 ESV

Why is it that when you least want to fall asleep
you do, and when you desperately want to you can't?
The unwelcome grip of sleep is like torture. When
sleep doesn't happen at night, staying awake in the day
becomes almost impossible. Being lulled to sleep at
the wrong time can be downright dangerous too, as
Eutychus discovered when the Apostle Paul talked for
a long time.

There is another type of sleep that's even more
dangerous than what Eutychus experienced. It's the kind
that dulls your senses to spiritual things. By renewing
and refreshing your spirit in Scriptures, you find new
calm and reassurance. Reviewing God's Word is a great
way to soothe your mind and heart. No matter the hour
of the day or night, the words of God bring rest.

God, I don't want to be lulled to sleep spiritually. Help me
to be more alert to what is going on around me.

I will sing
of your strength;
I will sing aloud
of your steadfast love
in the morning.

PSALM 59:16 ESV

Ask and Receive

*"Keep on asking, and you will receive what you ask for.
Keep on seeking, and you will find. Keep on knocking,
and the door will be opened to you."*

MATTHEW 7:7 NLT

The disciples had obviously asked God for many things before Jesus uttered these words. However, Jesus had been with them on earth. He had not yet accomplished on the cross what he came to earth to do, he had not stood as a mediator before God for you, the veil had not yet been torn, and the Holy Spirit had not been given to you.

Christ's death and resurrection provided the way for you to approach God because your sin has been forgiven. The Holy Spirit came to guide you in the way you should go, and he reforms your mind to be one with Christ. When you pray and your heart is aligned with Jesus, God will surely give you everything you need and fill your joy.

God, help me to ask for the right things. I want to know what is on your heart and to ask according to that. Thank you for sending a mediator so I am able to talk to you.

Encourage Others

Encourage one another and build each other up,
as you are already doing.

1 Thessalonians 5:11 csb

The events of life and the digression of the world should not shock you or cause you to panic. Instead, the realization that one day you will go home to Jesus should encourage you and reassure you through the dismal times. Share that encouragement with other believers so they too can be motivated to endure.

As you edify others, may it be with a heart that yearns to see them prosper in their life with the Lord. Each person is different, so how they get motivated will be different. Listen and learn from the Lord regarding his creations. Then, humbly serve other believers, provide them comfort, and spur them on in their faith.

God, please show me how I can encourage someone else
today. Thank you for the family you have adopted me into.

DAY 75

Wonderfully Made

I praise you because I am fearfully and wonderfully made;
your works are wonderful, I know that full well.
PSALM 139:14 NIV

The Father created you in his image for his purpose with much care and consideration. Be careful not to complain about the handiwork of God but to praise him for his wonderful design. He is worthy of admiration not resentment and criticism.

Taking care of yourself can be a way of respecting God for his gift, but rejecting the wonderful way he made you by hating who you are is unappreciative. Consider how the Lord delights in you and how he created you for his pleasure. Rather than comparing yourself to others, you can ask for his eyes to see the way he does. Revel in your unique and wonderful design while giving him all the glory and praise.

Father, thank you for how you have created me. You have made me wonderfully, and I want to be grateful for my uniqueness.

Everlasting Love

"I have loved you with an everlasting love;
I have drawn you with unfailing kindness."
JEREMIAH 31:3 NIV

The Israelites often turned away from God in favor of other idols or of themselves. Then, when they faced persecution, they would run back to him. Over and over, he took them back. He does not turn aside a contrite heart. True repentance should not present only when help is needed, but God understood the weakness of the Israelites and continued to welcome them home, showing them unfailing kindness.

Even when your faith is weak, God will accept you if you ask. He helps you to mature in faith and gives you ample amounts of grace. His love is everlasting and his compassion is certain. His mercy is undeniable. Thank him for forgiving your sins again and again, for calling you back to him, and for treating you as a true heir of his kingdom.

God, thank you for letting me come back to you over and over again. Your unfailing kindness amazes me.

There is great
freedom in admitting
your shortcomings
and allowing the
Father to be your
strength.

The Lord's Delight

His pleasure is not in the strength of the horse,
nor his delight in the legs of the warrior;
the LORD delights in those who fear him,
who put their hope in his unfailing love.
PSALM 147:10-11 NIV

God is not lacking in strength. He wants you to learn how to trust in him and rely on his might rather than attempt to muscle your way through life in your own strength. Humility is far more pleasing to him than your ability. Your skills and strength are gifts from God, and your humble love is your grateful gift back to him.

Both the mighty horse and the tender butterfly were created by God, both are cared for by God, and both reflect a side of his character. Even if you feel confident and capable, you ought to fear God and follow his leadership. This will be pleasing to him and will keep you out of a lot of trouble.

Thank you, God, for your tenderness and your strength.
Both have blessed my life in more ways than I can count.
I trust you with everything I have.

Condemnation

"Do not judge others, and you will not be judged. Do not condemn others, or it will all come back against you. Forgive others, and you will be forgiven."
LUKE 6:37 NLT

God requires his children to extend grace toward others, since he covered them with his grace. He proclaimed you innocent because Christ paid for your sins. Yet, if you judge others, then you choose to relinquish God's forgiving verdict of you. As soon as you condemn others by holding them to their sins, you condemn yourself, and all your sins will be held against you.

Don't overlook God's command on how you should love others. In doing so, you despise his love for you. His love is unchanging, but he will withhold his grace from those who withhold it from others. His Word is clear. The choice is yours.

God, help me not to judge others but to extend grace to them as you have to me. I want to live with an attitude of humility and forgiveness toward those around me.

Path of Life

*The path of the righteous is like the morning sun,
shining ever brighter till the full light of day.*

PROVERBS 4:18 NIV

The path to life can be treacherous at times. It may lead you to places you do not like to go. However, there is joy found in the journey. Not only are there eternal pleasures stored up for those who remain faithful, but there are rewards here now for following God. The greatest of these rewards is that you grow closer to God the more you walk with him. You understand his love, his character, and his plan better because you have a relationship with him.

Following God is the only path that leads to true and lasting life. When you stay the course, he fills you with joy, makes his presence known, and leads you every step of the way.

Thank you , Father, for the eternal pleasures you have promised to those who faithfully follow you. Help me see the brightness of your full light.

Protection

Let all who take refuge in you be glad;
let them ever sing for joy.
Spread your protection over them,
that those who love your name may rejoice in you.
PSALM 5:11 NIV

The remarkable grace God gives you provides impenetrable protection and insatiable joy! If you did not understand God, you would likely not appreciate his protection. You might fight against his laws and act out in disobedience. Then you would also be vulnerable to all the enemy's attacks and the elements of the world.

The Lord's protection does not guarantee that you will be spared from pain or sadness. It is a safety much more lasting, protecting your heart from failing and keeping your feet on the path that leads to life. Those who do not understand will attempt to build their own barricade, but those who realize what God's grace entails have every reason to rejoice.

God, thank you for your protection over my life. I rejoice in you because you are my joy.

DAY 81

The Great Escape

The LORD brought his people out of Egypt,
loaded with silver and gold;
and not one among the tribes of Israel even stumbled.
PSALM 105:37 NLT

The story of Israel's rescue from hundreds of years of slavery in Egypt is not to be thought of lightly. What a miracle that God's chosen people were finally delivered. There were generations after generations that were born and died in slavery, and finally this was the generation that God set free. Not only were they set free, but he loaded them up with silver and gold and made it easy for them to escape.

Sometimes these stories seem so far away in history that it's hard to relate to them. Remind yourself that God is the God of yesterday, today, and forever. He is as present this day as he was with his people hundreds of years ago. What a powerful God you serve!

God, when I need to escape into freedom, I pray that you would lead me. You are faithful and good, and I trust you to show me the way.

In His Arms

After taking them in his arms,
he laid his hands on them and blessed them.

MARK 10:16 CSB

The word *blessed* here comes from the Greek word *eulogeo*, which means either to celebrate or to consecrate. Whether you are parents or you take care of other children, you recognize that there is no way for you to perfectly protect and provide for them alone. Only God has true power and authority over their lives, so you have to consecrate them to him and trust that he cares for them even more than you can.

Jesus lived by example, and he has asked you to follow in his steps. He prioritized children, celebrated them, and even used them in his mission. Children are not a burden to Jesus but a blessing that he embraces. You can trust him with the children in your life.

God, help me to value the life of children. Whether they are mine or someone else's, you want them to be protected and provided for. Help me to bless them in whatever way they need in a given moment.

*Be strong and
let your heart
take courage,
All you who wait
for the Lord.*

PSALM 31:24 NASB

DAY 83

Not Destroyed

We are hard pressed on every side, but not crushed;
perplexed, but not in despair; persecuted, but not
abandoned; struck down, but not destroyed.
2 CORINTHIANS 4:8-9 NIV

You are God's treasure in a jar of clay. The Holy
Spirit lives in you and enables you to have the power to
accomplish all the Lord has called you to. This strength
did not originate with you but with the Spirit, so your
life testifies of God.

Just as jars of clay are, you may be battered and
bruised. You may even shatter! But the treasure that is
within you is unbreakable. No matter what happens,
you are not crushed, you do not need to despair, and
you are never abandoned. What God has fashioned
and redeemed cannot be destroyed.

Thank you, God, that you have made me indestructible. I
rely on your strength to walk through each day in spite of
the difficulties I face.

DAY 84

No More Tears

You have delivered my soul from death,
my eyes from tears, my feet from stumbling.
PSALM 116:8 ESV

God has promised his children a time where there
will be no more death, tears, or stumbling. This life is
full of hardships, but you can live in hope that a day will
come where joy will reign supreme. It is this hope that
carries you through the hard times, when you trust that
God is still good and that he has good plans for you.

Bravely face this day with joy concerning your
future. This life is not where it all ends! Look forward
to an eternity of joy. Thank God that even today he
can bring relief to your physical pain, healing to your
emotional pain, and restoration to your spiritual
weakness. Lean on him through the hard times, and he
will give you strength to live with eternity in mind.

God, I look forward to the day when there are no more
tears, crying, or pain. Thank you for the hope of your
wonderful promise of eternal joy.

Deep Contentment

*I don't say this out of need, for I have learned to be content
in whatever circumstances I find myself.*

PHILIPPIANS 4:11 CSB

You can close your eyes and rest with ease when
your world is in perfect harmony. Happiness is at your
fingertips, and your steps are light. In these seasons,
it is effortless to declare God's goodness. The struggle
comes when life isn't easy. When you are surrounded
by heartbreak and disappointment. When grief feels
suffocating, and hope seems so far away. When every
day feels impossible.

In these times true contentment is still in your
reach. Open up your eyes and your heart to it. When
you learn to see joy in every circumstance, you are
able to step bravely into each day. Your circumstances
do not define you; rather, joy becomes so rooted and
engrained in who you are that finding peace is second
nature. True contentment, God's genuine peace, cannot
be easily shaken.

*God, I want to be truly content no matter what my
circumstances are. I understand that only you can give me
the peace I seek. I ask for it today.*

DAY 86

Even Before That

Your eyes saw my unformed body;
all the days ordained for me were written in your book
before one of them came to be.

PSALM 139:16 NIV

You celebrate your birthday as the day that your fully formed body came into the world and you breathed your first breath. Birthdays mark the beginning of your life, but in this Scripture, God was celebrating you long before your birthday. He saw you before you were even formed; he knew that you were destined for life even before that first breath. What an amazing God! He is not only all-knowing, but ever personal.

Take courage and strength from the truth that you were destined from the beginning, and you have a wonderful purpose. Whatever you may be about to face, hold your head high and remember the one who created you for such a time as this.

Thank you, Father, for your total attention. You see me in a way that no one else can. And you love me. You have a purpose and plan for me that is greater than I can imagine.

Encouraging Bravery

When I am afraid, I will trust you.
I praise God for his word.
I trust God, so I am not afraid.
What can human beings do to me?
PSALM 56:3-4 NCV

Parents admonish their children not to be afraid. The older you get, the more there seems to be afraid of. Who can you encourage today, not by telling them not to be afraid, but by asking them to be brave? Asking people to mask their fear will only work temporarily. Asking them to make a choice for bravery gives them confidence in God's character and care.

Don't stuff down what you are feeling and move on in your own strength. Be brave in the situations that strike fear in you, knowing that God is fighting for you. Who needs to hear this today? Let God use you as his vessel to bring freedom. Help others remove their masks and hand them the bravery banner.

God, I want to walk in bravery and encourage others to do the same. Show me what I can do to conquer fear when it approaches.

More than You

Trust him at all times, you people;
pour out your hearts before him.
God is our refuge.
PSALM 62:8 CSB

It is great to spend time on your personal
relationship with God, yet there is more to your
faith than just yourself. God created you to be in
community with others. One really important benefit
of a close community is that you can be encouraged, or
encourage others, in times of distress.

Think of the last time you felt really anxious or
discouraged and reflect on who you were able to share
those feelings with. Together you can pour out your
hearts to him. Everyone is on this journey not just
individually, but walking alongside each other. Take
a moment today to encourage the people you are
walking with through life.

God, please show me how I can be intentional about
developing close relationships with those who encourage me
in my faith and with those whom I need to encourage.

Choose surrender
over control.
No problem
is too big for
God to handle.

Spiritual Destination

Blessed are those whose strength is in you,
whose hearts are set on pilgrimage.
PSALM 84:5 NIV

You never really arrive at your spiritual destination of holiness, and that's the way it is meant to be. The beauty is found where the heart is inclined toward finding the presence of God. This is your journey of faith in Christ. It is a pilgrimage in every sense of the word.

It might be a long and difficult terrain to navigate, but there will be wonders to see along the way and some profound insights and thoughts as you progress. This pilgrimage is one that ends at the most beautiful of places, one that your heart cannot fully comprehend. Enjoy the journey that you are on today.

God, I want to appreciate the beauty of my walk with you today. Show me how I can do that.

Uncomplicated Freedom

"I have swept away your offenses like a cloud,
your sins like the morning mist.
Return to me,
for I have redeemed you."
ISAIAH 44:22 NIV

Freedom in the Christian life can be over-complicated. You might try to find a way to humanize the redeeming work of the cross because you simply can't wrap your mind around the supernatural character of God.

It can be hard to understand the grace offered at Calvary because you are incapable of giving that kind of grace. But when God says that he has forgotten your sin, and that he has made you new, he really means it. God is love, and love keeps no record of wrongs. Nothing can keep you from his love. Salvation tore the veil that separated you from the holiness of God. That complete work cannot be diminished or erased.

God, thank you that freedom is truly simple. The beauty of the Gospel can be summed up in this single concept: grace, though undeserved, given without restraint. Help me to walk in this truth.

Powerful Virtues

*Do you despise the riches of his kindness, restraint,
and patience, not recognizing that God's kindness is
intended to lead you to repentance?*
ROMANS 2:4 CSB

Kindness, restraint, and patience are often thought
of as softer emotions. Consider however, the patience
of a mother giving birth, sacrificing her body and
emotions for the love of a child. Think of the kindness
of a sister who sits with her sibling in the darkest days
of depression. Think of a daughter who cares diligently
for her dying parent.

None of those actions are soft or meek. Kindness,
restraint, and patience can be fiercely, fervently, and
powerfully loving. God is exactly that: powerful
enough to lead you to change your ways and never
look back. This is nothing to think lightly of; it is life
changing!

*God, thank you for your kindness, restraint, and patience
that compel me to change my selfish ways and submit
myself to you.*

DAY 92

Surrender and Rest

"Come to me, all you who are weary and burdened, and I will give you rest. Take my yoke upon you and learn from me, for I am gentle and humble in heart, and you will find rest for your souls. For my yoke is easy and my burden is light."
MATTHEW 11:28-30 NIV

When you are faced with a problem, your first instinct might be to grab it and not let it go. You have this belief that if you hold onto it tightly, you have some sense of control. Often that sense is false. It creates anxiety and lets fear flourish. The more you struggle to hold on, the harder the situation becomes, and the more exhausting the fight.

The attitude God wants you to have toward your problems is one of bravery. He asks you to choose surrender over control. A huge part of that brave choice is having faith in him. By surrendering your fears and letting go of worry, you are trusting God. Relax your grip, lift your hands to the sky, and breathe. No problem is too big for God to handle. When you trust him, you can finally rest.

God, I trust you in every aspect of my life. I surrender it all—even the most difficult parts—to you.

Graciousness

Kindness to the poor is a loan to the LORD,
and he will give a reward to the lender.
PROVERBS 19:17 CSB

When you give to those who cannot repay you, it is as if you are giving straight to God. The way you demonstrate your love for the Lord is by loving others. When you are gracious, God will be gracious to you. When you forgive, God will forgive you. When you give without an expectation for compensation, he will certainly repay you for your faithfulness.

The Lord is tremendously generous; you cannot outgive him. He sees every good deed and will not forget the generosity and grace you show to others. Rather than looking for what you can get, consider what you can give. God will reveal to you the needs in others that he wants you to meet. And you can serve without expecting anything in return because God sees, and he will reward you.

God, who do you want me to give to today? I want to be sensitive to your leading and show others your incredible kindness.

The Good Lane

I am certain that I will see the LORD's goodness
in the land of the living.
PSALM 27:13 CSB

Do you ever catch yourself dwelling on the negative aspects of life? You may become quickly disinterested when someone tells you good news, but talk for hours about conflict, worries, and disappointment.

It is good to communicate things that aren't going so well in your life, but you can also fall into the trap of setting your mind on the wrong things. Give your mind over to truth and honor, pure and lovely things today. You are sure to find goodness in unexpected places! Thank God for creating you with goodness in your heart.

Father, help me to avoid the temptation of indulging in negative talk and harmful gossip today. I want to look for your goodness in everything.

When I am weak,
then I am strong.

2 Corinthians 12:10 nkjv

DAY 95

Don't Forget

*They soon forgot what he had done
and did not wait for his plan to unfold.*

PSALM 106:13 NIV

When you are asked about what you had for breakfast, can you even remember? With a mind that is often full, forgetfulness can threaten to derail your appointments, friendships, and even your relationship with Jesus. It's not that Jesus will ever depart from you, but if you quickly forget the good and gracious things he has done, you are less likely to spend time communicating with him.

In your moments of greatest joy, don't forget the source of that joy. Give yourself some space today to remember Jesus and what he has done in your life. Thank him for all the times he has provided you with wisdom, peace, and assurance.

God, I want to remember your goodness to me every day. Help me not to forget how much you have blessed me with.

Second Opinion

When my enemies retreat,
they stumble and perish before you.
PSALM 9:3 TPT

When you go to the doctor, you might not always be confident in their diagnosis. People will usually encourage you to get a second opinion. There may be times when significant people in your life have told you something about yourself that makes you feel terrible. They might have labelled you as selfish, or inconsiderate, or any number of accusations.

This is your time to get a second opinion. Go straight to your heavenly Father and ask him what he thinks. This is the God who created you and loves you unconditionally. He will show you who you really are.

God, thank you for seeing me for who I am—redeemed by you. Thank you for your voice of truth that combats the lies of others.

Gems

*Oil and incense bring joy to the heart,
and the sweetness of a friend is better than self-counsel.*
PROVERBS 27:9 CSB

When you sign up for a competitive team sport, you have a basic understanding that you're going to have to work hard and that emotions will run high to win. You know that you'll win some, you'll lose some, and that somewhere along the way you'll start to feel good about playing the game whether you win or lose.

Playing a competitive team sport can sometimes feel the same as building relationships with other women. You win some—forming incredible relationships—and lose some. You were created uniquely, and while you are asked to love others, it doesn't mean that you will form a best-friend relationship with each woman you meet. Cherish the sweet friends in your life today.

God, thank you for friends who hold me accountable but also lift me up when I need it. Bless them today. Let them know your nearness and your love.

DAY 98

Jesus Rep

Whatever you do, whether in word or deed, do it all in the name of the Lord Jesus, giving thanks to God the Father through him.

COLOSSIANS 3:17 NIV

When you work for a company or organization, you are expected to represent their brand. Organizations with a good reputation typically have a culture that their people are committed to being a part of. When you think of that company or brand, you can identify a certain value.

When you become a follower of Jesus, you also become his representative. Your personal relationship with Christ will inspire you to express something of his love, goodness, and grace to the world around you. You don't always need to shout that you are doing things in his name, you just need make sure your words and actions are influenced by his grace. Be encouraged as you represent him wherever you go.

God, I want to reflect you in the best possible way! Help me to live with an attitude of grace as I show your love to those around me.

Confident in Incompetence

It is not that we think we are qualified to do anything on our own. Our qualification comes from God.
2 Corinthians 3:5 nlt

Whether bringing a brand new baby home from the hospital, giving your first major presentation at work, or simply making your first Thanksgiving meal, there's probably been at least one moment in your life that had you thinking, *I have no idea what I'm doing. I'm not qualified.* Chances are, you put a smile on your face, dove in, and did your best anyway.

The older you get, the more you realize how truly helpless you are. But you also beautifully realize it's okay. There is great freedom in admitting your shortcomings and allowing the Father to be your strength. No matter what he asks of you, you are confident in your incompetence. You may not be capable, but God is more than qualified to carry out his plans through you.

Thank you, God, that you are my confidence. I can do whatever you call me to do because you are my strength.

DAY 100

Secure Feeling

*If you lie down, you will not be afraid;
when you lie down, your sleep will be sweet.*
Proverbs 3:24 esv

Sweet sleep. That goal after a day filled with hectic schedules and cramped expectations dissipates with the fast drumbeat of a fearful heart. You've probably been there, eyes wide-open staring into a dark room, ears strained for sound, and your breath held.

As you incorporate the Word of God into your life, God brings a different kind of security. Not the type you install with alarms or pay big money for, but the kind that underlies your thoughts and actions. Spend your last waking hours intentionally thinking through the blessings of your day. Remember God's faithfulness. Prepare for sweet sleep with confidence in God. Let truth relax your racing heart and taut muscles. When trust is anchored in a secure God, frightening insecurities fade.

God, thank you for being my security. Help me to rest in you and to find the sweet peace that I need in those moments I feel insecure.